Everything is PERFECT, Just not ME!

A Roadmap to Self-Acceptance

by:

Dr. Jane Tornatore

CONTENTS

Introduction

"Our first and last love is self-love." ~Christian Nestell Bovee

"Only I can change my life. No one can do it for me." ~Carol Burnett

"Well, I am totally screwed," I thought and closed the book. It was almost 20 years ago, and I had been reading a book by Wayne Dyer. He wrote about the power of our thoughts to create our life. He proposed the idea that if we think negative thoughts, our life will be negative. If we focus on the positive, our life will reflect that. The idea immediately depressed me; I had way too many negative thoughts and I didn't see any way to stop thinking them.

You see, I have this all-or-nothing, perfectionist personality. If I do something, I have to do it all the way and do it perfectly. As you might imagine, that gets in the way of actually getting anything done.

Yet, when I embraced the idea that little changes are enough, big changes started happening. I know, it may seem counterintuitive, but much of life is.

There is a reason I am passionate about helping people love themselves and how I know it is possible for you.

I remember not feeling good about myself from a very young age. I think I came out of the womb anxious. I grew up feeling like I didn't belong, even in my own family. I remember when I was about 5, planning how I was going to run away so my family wouldn't have to be "infected" by me. Strange thought for a 5-year-old, but there you have it. I remember that it was a very sunny day and the buttercups were in bloom. I didn't make it past a couple of blocks—I think it must have been lunchtime and my hunger won over my self-loathing.

I always had friends who loved me, but I could never quite figure out why. I remember a friend in college (who is still a good friend 35 years later) telling me "Jane, I wish you could see yourself as your friends see you." Actually, I had many friends say that to me. What were they seeing that I wasn't?

I've always been told I have many good qualities, but I could never believe the tellers. Or I could see I had those qualities, but inwardly believed I should be BETTER than I was, so the good qualities didn't count. Does any of this sound familiar to you?

You can see why I developed tools for self-compassion. To gather them, I sought out therapy, group work, meditation, seminars, coaching, training programs, and a bunch of self-help books.

Because I am a recovering perfectionist, I also needed to hav some serious academic credentials to go along with all the personal work I have done. I earned a Master's degree from the University of Illinois in Human Development and Family Studies and a PhD from the University of Minnesota in Family Social Science with added specializations in Family Therapy and Teaching. If you have any questions on how to study with unmedicated ADHD, I'm your woman.

I have been a therapist in private practice since 2005. I have helped hundreds of people pay less attention to that yammering committee of nasty voices in their head telling them they are not enough. I believe I can help you also. I figure if these tools can help me, they can help almost anyone.

Self-acceptance and being kind to ourselves sound good, but few of us actually practice these things. Change is scary. Even good change is scary! The goal of this book is to suggest tiny changes to make the journey to self-acceptance less frightening. This book is designed to circumvent our resistance by taking small steps instead of giant leaps of change all at once. Although they may seem insignificant, these small changes will lead to self-compassion.

Change doesn't happen by reading books, thinking about it, understanding it, or applying logic. Change happens by taking small actions, one at a time.

Many of us have in our heads what a colleague of mine, Dr. Kristen Allott, refers to as "The Committee." This committee tells us self-sabotaging thoughts. It says things like, "I've tried it a couple of times and my life is not different. This isn't going to work for me."

This might be the number one way our ego stops us from trying new things. These thoughts are why we give up diets after a few weeks or a few days, or stop exercising, or eating better, or continuing anything that requires sustained effort to create a change.

The hard truth is that our ego does not like any change, even if it is a change that will make our life better, and we want it to happen.

This is where we tap into our desire and remind ourselves why we want to create this change. Our willpower sucks, but our desire is boundless, if we tap into it.

Perhaps The Committee says, "This is going to take more time and effort than I have energy for."

This may actually be true, if we believe it to be so. What we forget is that we have choices about how to use our time and energy.

There is a story about a college professor who did a demonstration for her students. On a table in the front of the lecture hall, there was a grocery bag and a clear glass jar filled to the top with rocks. She asked her students if there was any more room in the jar. They all agreed that there was no more room in the jar. Then the professor pulled a bag of pebbles out of the grocery bag. She slowly poured pebbles into the jar until it was filled to the top. Once again, she asked the students if the jar was full. Once again, they all agreed it was. Next, the professor pulled out a bag of sand. The students began to murmur to themselves. She emptied the bag of sand into the jar. This time, before she even finished asking the question, the students allowed there was probably still some room left in the jar. Her point was made, but to drive it home, she pulled out a small jar of water and emptied it into the jar full of rocks, pebbles, and sand.

Can you guess what she was trying to convey to her students? If we don't put the important things in our life first, we won' have room for them. If she had filled the jar with even just the pebbles, there would not have been enough room for the bigger rocks.

The problem is, we fill our lives with the little activities we "should" do, and we never have room for those things in our life that make our life meaningful. How many of us put our self-nurturing at the bottom of the list?

When you make self-care actions a priority, your life can be filled with the self-compassion you want.

What my clients and I have discovered is that when we are nurtured, we are more able to do the other things in our life with less stress and more energy.

I've found in my practice that people really struggle with self-worth when it comes to making changes. Making changes, even good changes, can be painful for our psyche. Humans are creatures of habit, and the only way to bring about change on a deeper level is consistent and persistent practice. My purpose for writing this book is to help you move through the fear that naturally comes when we try to love ourselves more. I want to give you the tools to make the changes you've wanted to make for years, but perhaps you don't feel you deserve.

So, find a comfy spot on your couch, wrap yourself in a cozy blanket, grab a cup of tea, and give yourself the gift of reading this book to learn how to love yourself. I promise, you deserve it.

One

Our Brain Is a Scary Place: Why We Struggle So Much

"It can be an effort to be positive. It is worth the effort." ~Jane Tornatore

Yes, your brain is a scary place. Luckily, humans have been studying the brain and how it works for decades, so we have some understanding of what goes on in there and how to change it.

Velcro versus Teflon

I would like to tell you about a way to understand why some thoughts seem to affect us more than others. It's called the

"Negativity Bias" and it's often described as "Velcro vs Teflon" in our brain. I first came across this concept from Dr. Rick Hanson. (If you want a wonderful book to help you understand how our brain works and how to make changes for more peace of mind, read his book *Hardwiring Happiness*.) In our brains, negative thoughts, comments, and events stick like velcro, whereas compliments slide out of our minds like teflon. Think about this: how much do you dwell on compliments versus criticism?

Back in the days of saber-toothed tigers, life was about survival. One simply could not spend their days luxuriously laying around with no cares in the world. The people who worried were the ones who stayed alive.

The worriers worried about many things, like which plants were edible and which were poisonous. They worried about neighboring groups and wild animals. They worried about shelter and sustenance. The worriers survived because they were always looking for dangerous things to avoid and important things to remember.

Many generations later, we get the benefit of their evolutionary brains. The worriers passed on their worrying genes. Our primordial ancestors that laid around and enjoyed life instead of worrying didn't last long. Yay for the worriers!

So, in this current day, is worrying still useful? Yes, when it moves us to action. Human beings are designed to spot the problems and come up with solutions, to look for danger, and to avoid hazards at all costs. Our brain works well for survival, but it falls short when it comes to self-love and compassion. We are basically programmed to look for the negative to protect ourselves from harm. All this anxious thinking doesn't bode well for making positive changes, unless we are motivated and persevere.

Neural Network Pathways

In 1949, Donald Hebb, a Canadian neuropsychologist known for his work in the field of associative learning, coined the phrase, "neurons that fire together, wire together." What does that mean, exactly? Every single action, thought, behavior, and belief is simply a pattern of neural networks firing in the brain.

We group thoughts and memories in our brain in ways similar to file folders on your computer screen. Things in related categories are grouped together. For example, if we are thinking about a family member, it becomes easier to have memories or thoughts about other family members. It is harder to switch gears and think about math problems while strolling down memory lane.

We can use what we know about neural networks to make NEW neural networks and learn to override our ancient worrier brain mode (or at least recognize it, so it doesn't have to be in control.) This is what the rest of this book is about.

Two

The Feelings Model: How to Make Your Feelings Not So Scary

"When you know how to notice and stay with an uncomfortable experience you have true freedom. You are not compelled by your conditioning to need things to be a certain way for you to feel ok."
~Susan Campbell

"If you are going through hell, keep going." ~Winston Churchill

"What you resist, persists." ~Richard Paterson

I would like to start this chapter with a story about a very disgruntled woman—me. A few years back, a massage herapist friend of mine was offering a package deal. I rarely give myself the gift of massage. It is a block I have about elf-care. (Don't worry, I'm working on it.)

My friend was offering an excellent deal; the massages were half price and had to be used within 6 months. I bought 3 and went for my first one. It was wonderful! Then, summer came and I got busy and forgot all about it. Months went by, and I remembered. I called my friend and asked when the package expired. She told me I had one week left! I quickly jumped online to try to find a time on her calendar, but she was booked solid.

'll admit it; I threw myself a pity party. My inner mean voice immediately piped in and started fussing. "I should've never wasted that money." "She should've let me know the time was almost up." "I should've made these appointments months ago! I'm so stupid, why do I do things like this?" My inner monologue was pretty brutal at this point.

stewed in my frustration with myself and the situation until t dawned on me what was happening. I was REPRESSING my emotions and NOT feeling them. As I came up with very excuse in my brain to blame my friend or me, I realized he excuses were a shield my committee was using to have me ocus on anything but my actual feelings of anger. In my amily of origin, anger was associated with scary things and people got hurt. I had spent my life trying to avoid outright nger.

I still remember that moment; I was standing in my kitchen staring at my sink. I decided to just sit with the anger and feel it. It was a crappy situation which I could do nothing about, and I was pissed-off. I went to my couch and sat down. After a few minutes, the anger started to subside and I began to feel better. I realized, as relief washed over me, that feeling my feelings was actually more helpful than repressing them. I actually felt...better!

My friend texted me 30 minutes later, offering to extend the timeframe. I immediately scheduled both massages. It was an easy lesson that ended well, but it definitely got me thinking about how my brain reacted to strong feelings and what actually helps me move through them.

That's when I formulated what I call my "Feelings Model."

The Feelings Model

We do three things with our feelings:

REPRESS: We hold back the flood of emotions as it comes, building pressure and tension.

FEEL: We move through the emotion by feeling it and letting the neurochemicals in our brain do their job.

FEED: We perpetuate the feeling by thinking negative thoughts such as "I should have known better" or "Of *course* I'm mad—she screwed up!"

Think of a reservoir that holds water. The reservoir has a source of water going in, and the dam keeps all the water from flowing downriver. If everything is working naturally, the water comes in from the source and when the dam gets full, the extra water flows over the dam.

When we repress our feelings, we are making the dam higher, and emotions begin building up, increasing the pressure. When we feed these emotions with negative thoughts, we're pouring a waterfall into the reservoir, continuing to build pressure.

Those futile attempts we make to not feel actually make the feelings stick around. When we just feel them, the emotions flow, like the water pouring into the reservoir, over the dam, and into the river to flow away gently.

Dr. Jill Bolte Taylor, a brain scientist, author, and Ted Talk speaker, talks about the 90-second rule for our body's chemical response to an emotion-triggering thought. According to Dr. Bolte Taylor, a thought triggers our brain to release a chemical component of our emotion, say jealousy. Within 90 seconds of the initial trigger, the chemical component of jealousy is gone from our blood, and the automatic response is complete. (I have also read it takes up to two minutes for this response to finish.) If we remain jealous, it is because we are feeding the emotion with more thoughts.

For a very strong emotion, the fastest I have gotten at letting my body's chemical response do its job, without repressing or feeding it, is five minutes. I practice the "progress, not perfection" motto! Five minutes may feel like a long time, but in actuality, it's a small part of your day.

Instead of stewing in your emotions, the remedy is simply just to **pay attention to what is happening in your body**. When you pay attention to your body, it brings more of your brain on board. When we are stressed, much of our brain shuts down and our lizard-brain, the part responsible for fight or flight, is in charge. You can tell this technique is really working when you notice your thoughts have shifted from what you were originally feeling to what's happening in your body as a result.

Take a moment to think about something that really bothers you. Notice how your body is responding to your thoughts. Is your heart beating normally or thumping hard? Do you feel your chest constricting or are you breathing normally? Do you feel any tingling anywhere? Do you have an upset stomach? Where are you holding tension? Don't try to change anything, just sit quietly and pay attention.

In keeping with our water theme, there is something Tara

Brach, psychologist and proponent of Buddhist meditation, talks about that I have named the Riverbed Awareness Model. (If you don't know Tara Brach, check out her books or YouTube videos. They are fabulous for helping increase self-compassion.)

In the Riverbed Awareness Model, you are the riverbed, and your feelings are the water.

Sometimes our feelings are so intense and consuming that we get confused and think the water is us, when in actuality, we are the riverbed, allowing emotions to flow through us. Sometimes the water is turbulent and sometimes it is slow. Like the riverbed, we are the container for our feelings. We are the ones holding these feelings and controlling the flow. We have the capacity to hold whatever is happening to us.

Often, we repress our emotions because we believe we don't have the capacity to hold our feelings. Consciously or unconsciously, we believe our feelings will kill us or stay forever. Taking the time to check in with your body helps you slow down enough for you to quietly begin to move past the intense emotions you are experiencing.

Tools to Help Feelings Be Less Overwhelming

Try these exercises the next time your emotions feel overwhelming:

- Remind yourself that feelings are just feelings, not reality. They are simply a physical sensation in your body.
- Label your feelings. Labeling helps reduce the intensity of emotions because it brings your frontal cortex (the decision-making and social behavior part of the brain) online and quiets the amygdala (the fight or-flight part of the brain).
- Pay attention to what your emotions feel like in your body. Notice how they always change. Emotions are not permanent; remember the 90-second rule. Feelings don't stay stagnant, they may ramp up or down within a short time. It's a powerful reminder that things are always capable of changing, and they won't stay the same forever. Realizing that something isn't going to last indefinitely is a great way to find the willingness to walk through it, knowing there IS another side.

Three

Change These Words,
Change Your Mind

"Stop shoulding on yourself." ~Albert Ellis

"Sticks and stones may break my bones, but words hurt over and over again." ~Unknown

Much of our stress is created by the words we use when we talk to ourselves. Here is a fabulous tool to start changing our thoughts, one at a time:

If I were Queen of the World I would ban these words:

- "Should"

- "Must"
- "Have to"
- "Need"
- And for Midwesterners, "Gotta."

Why? Because they make us feel bad. They have the opposite effect of what we intend. These words create resistance, internal struggle, and stress. Our ego hates not having a choice. When we perceive no choice, we resist, which creates more stress.

I would replace the banned words with:
- "It would be a good idea to..."
- "It would be helpful to..."
- "An option is to…"
- "I can choose to..."
- "I get to..."
- Only if it is really true… "I would like to..." and "I want to…"

Your thoughts are powerful. They might be the single most important predictor of your happiness. Yes, even more than your experiences.

Whether you believe that statement is true or not, this IS true…we sometimes can't control what happens to us in life, but we can control how we respond to what happens to us. Our thoughts are a huge part of our response.

Shawn Achor, author of the New York Times best-selling *The Happiness Advantage,* writes about many research studies that show how we think about our life changes how we respond to our life. How you talk to yourself MATTERS.

Before you get all freaked out about how many of your thoughts are negative, or mean, or just plain wrong, I assure you the goal is not to change all of your thoughts forever and ever to perfect, happy, and supportive thoughts. The goal is to make your thoughts a little less stressful and a little more helpful.

We have at least 10,000 thoughts a day. Of those, 80-90% are repetitive, and 70-80% of those thoughts are believed to be negative. No wonder so many of us walk around feeling stressed! If you start changing your thoughts, just think of the impact you can have on how you feel.

The problem is we have learned that telling ourselves we have no choice is the best way to motivate ourselves. It may be a way to motivate ourselves, but it doesn't work as well as we believe.

Think about it. How many times have you told yourself you have to do something, and then you don't do it? Why do we believe this method works? Because we see everyone else doing it and every once in a while it does work. If I am looking for a tool to help me, I want it to work more than every once in a while. No method works 100% of the time, but we want it to be effective most of the time.

Try this experiment: Do the exercise below and notice how often it works compared to your old method of beating yourself up. This requires paying attention and diligent awareness. Yes, it takes effort. But if you have, at the minimum, 10,000 thoughts a day, can you imagine the impact if you start shifting them? One thought at a time…

The "Change These Words, Change Your Mind" Tool

You have something you need to do or should have done already, right? Think of that thing, and say, "I should _____" or "I need to _____," out loud if possible. Close your eyes and notice what you feel in your body.

Most people feel tension, tightness, dread, heaviness, sometimes a sick feeling in their stomach. What do you feel?

Now choose one of these alternatives:

"It would be a good idea to…"
"It would be helpful to…"
"An option is…"
"I can…"
Or, if it's really true, "I want to…" or "I would like to…"

Think of that same thing you just spoke of, and use one of the alternatives instead of the banned words. I suggest, "It would be a good idea to _____" or "It would be helpful to _____." Go ahead and say it out loud, close your eyes, and notice what you feel in your body, and notice where you feel it. I mean what you physically feel, not just labeling it "better" or "good."

Most people notice they feel lighter or less tense. They feel like the task is more possible.

The very first time I presented this at a workshop on stress, a friend of mine who was in the audience, called me the next day and told me she had tried this exercise. She worked from home and she told herself she should do a task for work. She remembered the tool and said, "I want to make this sales call." She realized she didn't. So she didn't do it. She called me to tell me how good that decision felt. She did something else in that moment. Later on, she did the original task, but she did it with much less resentment. Success!

Part of the power of this tool is that it changes your perception while you are doing the things you are doing. It helps you be more at peace with what you are choosing to do, rather than resistant.

Four

Gratitude - The Most Powerful Tool In Your Toolbox

"It's not what you see is what you get. It's HOW you see is what you get." ~Warren Macdonald

"There is no lack of things to be grateful for if you remember to pay attention." ~Jen Sincero

What is gratitude exactly? Well, Merriam-Webster online defines it as "the state of being grateful; thankfulness." That's a pretty cool feeling to experience!

Why is gratitude so important?

Positive emotions fill our brain with dopamine and serotonin. These chemicals make us feel good and increase our ability to learn. They help us process new information, keep that information in the brain longer, and remember it faster later on.

In *The Happiness Advantage,* Achor presents study after study on how being primed to feel happy improves our ability to perform tasks and solve problems.

Not only that, we *feel* better when we think happy thoughts. People who are grateful are more energetic and emotionally intelligent. Gratitude is powerful!

Our neural pathways can be rewired faster if we have a feeling attached to the thoughts, as it uses more of our brain. Feeling and thinking employ different parts of the brain.

Many years ago, I decided to try out this gratitude thing. It sounded good, but I always test things on myself to see if they work before I share them with my clients. After 2-4 weeks of a daily gratitude practice, I noticed I started feeling spontaneously grateful throughout the day. It actually caught me by surprise! I could tell my neural pathways were being built and strengthened.

I recall once, when I was very stressed and on the hamster wheel of worry, I tried to feel gratitude as a solution. I could!

I realized I could hold both the stressful thought and gratitude at the same time, and that gratitude actually helped lessen the stress! By spending just a little time during the day focusing on gratitude, I was able to cope better in every aspect of my life. I was also experiencing the warmth of well being that comes from feeling truly grateful. And I was the one creating it!

So, what's the best way to practice gratitude? Yes, it's a practice. It's impossible to be perfectly grateful all the time; our brains are not wired to stay that way. We make the choice to create new gratitude-oriented neural pathways to replace some old self-defeating ones!

Here are two simple exercises you can do to help retrain your brain into grateful thinking:

Gratitude Practices

- List 3 things for which you are grateful.

- Spend 30 seconds FEELING gratitude. Pay attention to what is happening in your body. Do you feel chest expanding? Do you feel it becoming bigger and warmer?

Some people prefer lists, either written or spoken aloud. They can include the same things over and over again, or they can be as varied as you'd like.

My favorite way to focus on gratitude is to FEEL it viscerally. By noticing what is changing in my body, I'm creating awareness of what the gratitude is doing to my body. I tend to notice my face relaxing, maybe a small smile, a warmth in my chest. My breathing tends to be even and comfortable. I don't even need to list things for which I am grateful anymore. I have so many gratitude neural pathways that the feeling is easy to create. Woohoo!

Another helpful tool is to find a Gratitude Celebration Partner. You can come up with your own fun title for this person. Spend 1-5 minutes a day sharing your gratitude with your partner and celebrating theirs. Any mode of communication works here, texting, phone calls, emails—whatever works. Be a cheerleader for one another and find yourself being grateful for your partner too. You are lucky to have someone willing to share your joy!

When Is a Good Time to Do Your Gratitude Practice?

Upon waking, your brain starts to come online. Your neural pathways fire and plans for the day begin to materialize. This is a powerful time to introduce gratitude into your day. As you picture the events of your day unfolding, infusing a feeling of gratefulness helps start your day off in a positive light. If you start your day with gratitude, gratitude will come up more naturally without you consistently trying!

Another important time to focus on gratitude is in the evening, as you get ready to sleep. When you sleep, your brain stores and categorizes the events of the day. If you're thinking or feeling gratitude before sleep, your memories are influenced, and are more likely to have gratitude incorporated into them.

Morning gratitude sets you up for your day, and bedtime thinking shapes how you perceive the experiences in your life. Both are important. Feel free to award yourself plenty of bonus points if you practice morning and night!

These waking up/planning and unwinding/categorizing processes are already happening because of our biology; we just get to inject gratitude. Think of it as a life-hack! We are adding joy and happiness simply by adding gratitude into these already occurring processes.

The trickiest part of this exercise is consistency. Humans tend to feel better and then stop doing the very thing that helped them. Consistency is key here. If you miss a day (or week, or month), pick right back up as soon as you remember. While the time of day is an important factor, the most important part is the actual feeling. You can take 30 seconds at any point during the day to feel gratitude!

Five

Hello, Gorgeous!

"Your path to love is not to seek for love, but merely to seek and find all the barriers within yourself you have built against it." ~Rumi

This last practice I share is powerful. It is also the tool that brings up the greatest resistance. Stay with me, it's worth it!

I'm using "gorgeous" here because that is what I learned and it works for me. Use any word that feels powerful and celebrates the body you have. Some alternatives are: capable, handsome, powerful, strong, healthy, beautiful, and magnificent. I believe we all fit these descriptors, even if we don't yet see it.

I discovered this habit in my early 40's, when I attended a self-help talk given by woman in her sixties. She was sharing with us how she learned to love herself. Every morning she would get out of bed, naked, stand in front of a full-length mirror, throw out her arms and say "Hello, Gorgeous!"

Well, I had issues with my body and I was appalled. She wasn't young, she wasn't slim, and yet she had the audacity to say "Hello, Gorgeous" to herself and mean it! I was horrified and intrigued. I realized the value of this woman celebrating herself even though she didn't fit what our society views as "perfect." As a perfectionist, that blew my mind.

The next morning I tried it. I reached up my arms, said "Hello, Gorgeous" and immediately collapsed inward. It brought up self-loathing and self-judgment. I understood my resistance was a result of negative messages I had internalized, and I wanted to overcome them. I kept at it, and gradually felt more and more confident greeting myself. As I write this, I am almost 57, and every day I appreciate my naked body in the mirror. I am grateful.

During the writing of this book, one morning I stood in front of my bedroom mirror and blurted out, "Hello, Love!" instead of "gorgeous." I was surprised, and it felt right and good. Now I say whichever phrase I want to in the morning

My advice to you is to sit with the resistance and do it anyway. It's just three seconds. It's a SMALL practice with a big impact. If you keep moving through your resistance, you will eventually work through those beliefs that keep you from feeling lovable or worthy of appreciation.

When I first started my "Hello, Gorgeous" practice, I would seek out places of my body to criticize. It took a long time for me to look in the mirror and not immediately start seeing flaws.

I gave this exercise to a client who found it too hard and overwhelming, so she decided to start small -- she began by focusing on her eyes. You can do this too! If your whole body is too much for you, pick out a part you like and give yourself a moment to appreciate that part of you.

Human brains are wired to look for what's wrong. By doing this exercise, you are rewiring your brain to shift your focus from what's wrong to what's right, from criticism to appreciation—but keep at it!

Maybe you're in a better place and don't have to work as hard as I did on this. No matter where you are starting from, try to greet that image in the mirror as a friend and not an enemy, as a human whose life story is written on your body in the form of scars, stretch marks, wrinkles, moles, freckles, and soft places. Today, look in the mirror and give your reflection the grace and admiration it deserves!

Six

Do Unto Yourself
as You Would Do Unto Others

"Self-love is not selfishness. Love is the cure of selfishness." ~Bishop Michael Curry

"...self care is never a selfish act—it is simply good stewardship of the only gift I have, the gift I was put on the earth to offer to others." ~Parker Palmer

I'm going to share with you what may sound like a radical idea: Self-love isn't selfish. Self-love is actually self-compassion and it makes the world a better place.

It sounds crazy, doesn't it?

People are scared to go on the journey to love themselves more because we've been taught it's selfish. We all know that being selfish is BAD and to be avoided at all costs.

Over and over again, what I've found to be true for both myself and my clients, is that when we love ourselves more, we are kinder to others in our life. We become more generous, patient, and kind. Many of us fear if we love ourselves more, we will somehow morph into a selfish hedonist and end up hurting people we care about. I have found the exact opposite to be true. We are able to give more to the people we love and to the world when we love ourselves. I promise.

I've never had a person say to me, "Now that I'm kinder to myself, I'm mean as all get out to everyone else." What they actually find is that they are more present, patient, gentle, kind, and loving.

I ask you to embrace the idea that self-acceptance is a proactive way to make the world a better place. The more love you pour into yourself, the more you have to pour into others! You, and the world, deserve it.

I will leave you with my personal credo. You are welcome to use it, embrace it, print it out and put it on your wall, whatever you want!

When people love themselves, they don't judge others. The more they love themselves, the better boundaries they have. They teach others love by example, not by telling. People who love themselves show others what is possible—kindness, love, acceptance, and forgiveness. I want that for you, me, and everyone we meet.

~ *Dr Jane Tornatore*

About the Author

In college, Jane's motto was "writing is the bane of my life." Not the best motto for an English major. She went on to earn a Master's degree at the University of Illinois and a PhD at the University of Minnesota.   Apparently, she learned at an early age not to believe ALL her negative thoughts.

Dr Jane Tornatore, LMFT, is a therapist, speaker, and author based in Seattle, WA. She has been in private practice since 2005. Her style incorporates compassion, curiosity, deep listening, and heartfelt optimism, along with powerful shots of playfulness.

Jane adores her job because she gets to love and accept in her clients what they don't YET love and accept. She has the honor of witnessing them as they learn to love and accept themselves.

Jane has dedicated her career, and her life, to helping people love themselves and have self-compassion.

Dr. Jane sees clients in her private practice and online group coaching programs. Please visit www.doctortornatore.com or www.everydaylove.me for more information or contact us any time at hello@everydaylove.me.

Your journey to self-acceptance continues here!

Acknowledgments

"Now that you don't have to be perfect, you can be good." ~John Steinbeck

I would not have written this book without the fierce courage and encouragement of many, many people.

I have unending appreciation and awe for my clients and group members. It is the work they do inside and outside our sessions that inspires me to face my fears and trust that what I share will help others. Thank you from my heart.

To Andrea and Ellen, who both loved my blog posts and kept telling me people would be helped by what I have to say.

To Fabienne Fredrickson and Dolores Hirschmann, thank you for your inspiration, coaching, and love.

To JessAnn, Jen, Alice, Jeewon, and Rob—you have seen my value consistently since the 1980's, when I didn't. From you I started to believe that perhaps I *was* nifty.

To Adam, you, more than anyone on this planet, have helped

ne be more loving and self-accepting.

To Mary, your dance created the space for me to move my body to self-love and gave me a group of friends that rocked my world.

To M, my star-sister. You helped me feel less weird and less alone. I know you always have my back.

To my family members, who have loved me forever, and here are a lot of you! Special mention goes to Mom, who encouraged me to expand my mind and my world, and who was always excited about whatever I was doing, and to my sister Susie, who defines "unconditional love."

Lora Denton, you made writing this book fun. Your comments like "I love this book!" kept me excited and motivated and helped me when my doubts crept in. And your tattoos are the best!

What Dr. Jane's Clients Are Saying...

"I never thought I could change these feelings of not being good enough, nervousness around people, and lack of confidence. I saw no way to ever change it…and it has changed."

"I see myself using my brain differently and not being a victim. Instead I'm taking charge, being the powerful person I am. I'm really enjoying that I have freedom to make decisions and choose my moments. I didn't know I had a choice. It's important for me to notice I can learn this stuff. This is going to carry over into everything I do. I want to celebrate what I can do, and that's being me!"

"Since 2009, Dr. Jane Tornatore has been critically helpful and motivating to me through her group workshops. This book is more of the same intriguing teachings. Her ideas on how to grow my self-compassion were a huge help in fighting shame, setting better boundaries, and getting past resentments. Read this book, listen closely, and with tiny steps, act upon the concepts. That is my advice!"

"When I came in, I felt like I was drowning and being pulled down, and now I'm happy. I just feel so much lighter. I don't feel as overwhelmed. I feel like I have a path forward.'

"I am so happy with how I am doing and am feeling better and better after each session. I think (my partner) is also benefiting a lot from my reduced stress and the information we share about what I learn. Thank you for the tremendous gift of perspective, good advice, a kind ear, and all that you do."

"Jane has helped me find my authentic voice so I can become more successful in following my own path to happiness. In our talks she facilitated discussions where I became more aware of my true needs and wants, and was more successful at being authentic and having better self-realization. As a result, I made better decisions about what was best for me."

"I truly feel that Jane helped me in the best way. I would go back and ask her for help again. I have a much better outlook on my life and life in general from working through things with Jane and would recommend her to anyone that has lost their direction. It helped me a lot."

I'm learning I have a life to live. It is influenced by emotions and fear. They will always be there. I have a choice to be frightened or to embrace them and keep going; new ones will come. When I first came here, I was stuck in my thoughts. I'm learning to have greater peace. When you have peace your soul is satisfied. You can take what comes at you. You are not defensive…It allows me to be who I am— who I want to be."

"I soooo appreciate your authenticity; how you create a container that honors our equality and you demonstrate your deep commitment to honoring what's real, true and deep for you emotionally. Your presence and depth created such a safe container, modeling for us how to allow and access our own presence and depth. I love how you created ritual and exercises for us to feel and express, and how you modeled these things by showing us your depth and your humanness. Thank you for burning away the chaff to cut through to the core of what's real and true, for sharing from your heart in our group, with clear emotions. You modeled for me the courage to be with what's deep, raw, real, and true."

"Thank you! I am grateful for the work you do in these groups, in the world, and in your own personal life! Thank you for being a pioneer. :-)"

"I am so much better at taking care of myself and knowing my limits. I trust myself and my ability to navigate my life...my vulnerability doesn't scare me as much as it used to. It feels good to not feel so afraid."

59010174R10029

Made in the USA
Columbia, SC
30 May 2019